ĤF421148

101 FACTS ABOUT LIONEL MESSI THAT EVERY KID NEEDS TO KNOW!

Discover Fun Facts and Amazing Adventures of The World's Favorite Soccer Star

R. Parlour

Hey Messi Fans! Are you ready to embark on an exciting adventure into the incredible world of Lionel Messi? This book is bursting with amazing and fun facts about your favorite football superstar that will make you admire him even more! Some of these facts you might already know, but others will surprise and delight you.

Did you know Messi started playing football when he was just a little boy in Rosario, Argentina? Or that he overcame a growth hormone deficiency to become one of the greatest players ever? Messi loves spending time with his family and has a playful dog named Hulk who often joins him on the field. He was the first player to score in six different club competitions in a single season with Barcelona. How amazing is that?

This book is filled with stories about Messi's life, from his humble beginnings to his incredible achievements on the biggest stages, like winning the FIFA World Cup and earning countless Ballon d'Or awards. You'll discover how Messi's magical dribbles, unstoppable goals, and teamwork made him a legend. You'll also learn about his generous heart, as he uses his success to help others through his foundation and inspire millions of young players around the world to chase their dreams.

So, grab your favorite snack, get cozy, and join us on this thrilling journey to learn all about Lionel Messi. Let's see how many of these fun facts you already know and which ones will become your new favorites!

Are you ready to see Lionel Messi's incredible skills in action? Scan the QR code below to watch a special video of **Messi's Top 25 Goals ever** scored for Barcelona! You'll witness amazing dribbles, stunning goals, and unforgettable moments that make Messi a true superstar. Grab a tablet or smartphone, scan the code, and dive into the excitement of one of the greatest footballers ever. Get ready to cheer and be inspired by Messi's amazing talents!

Enjoy the magic of Messi and let his amazing goals inspire you to chase your own dreams!

1
EARLY BEGINNINGS IN ROSARIO

Lionel Andrés Messi was born on June 24, 1987, in the city of Rosario, Argentina. Growing up in a modest neighborhood, he was the third of four children in a tight-knit family. From a very young age, Messi showed a deep love for football, often playing with his older brothers and cousins in the streets. His grandmother Celia was one of the first to recognize his exceptional talent and encouraged him to pursue the sport seriously. Tragically, she passed away when he was just ten, but her influence on him remains strong.

2
THE NICKNAME "LA PULGA"

Messi is affectionately known as "La Pulga," which means "The Flea" in Spanish. This nickname originated because he was smaller than most of his peers but possessed incredible speed and agility. His low center of gravity allows him to change direction quickly, making it difficult for defenders to keep up. Just like a flea, he's quick, elusive, and almost impossible to catch! This nickname has stuck with him throughout his career, symbolizing his ability to make a massive impact despite his smaller stature.

3

A GROWTH HORMONE CHALLENGE

When Messi was just 10 years old, he was diagnosed with a growth hormone deficiency, a medical condition that hindered his physical development and required expensive treatment. Despite the financial strain, his parents were determined to support his dreams. As Messi's condition threatened to derail his football career, his family sought opportunities abroad. Their search for a solution eventually led them to FC Barcelona, a club that recognized Messi's potential and was willing to invest in his talent by covering his medical expenses. This set the stage for his ascent to global stardom.

4
A BIG MOVE TO BARCELONA

At the tender age of 13, Messi's life took a dramatic turn when he moved from Rosario, Argentina, to Barcelona, Spain, to join FC Barcelona's esteemed youth academy, La Masia. The move was a significant sacrifice for the young Messi and his family, who left behind their home, extended family, and familiar surroundings. Despite these obstacles, he thrived at La Masia, where he honed his technical abilities, tactical understanding, and embraced the club's philosophy of teamwork and humility.

Messi made his official debut for FC Barcelona's first team on October 16, 2004, in a derby match against Espanyol. At just 17 years, 3 months, and 22 days old, he became one of the youngest players ever to play for the club's senior team. Coming on as a substitute, his appearance was brief but electrifying; he showcased glimpses of his extraordinary talent, leaving fans eager for more. From that moment, it was clear that Messi was not just another promising player but a generational talent destined to make history.

6
FIRST GOAL FOR BARCELONA

Messi scored his first official goal for Barcelona on May 1, 2005, in a La Liga match against Albacete at the Camp Nou stadium. Entering the game as a substitute in the 88th minute, he quickly made an impact. In the 90th minute, he received a clever lobbed pass from Ronaldinho, controlled it deftly, and chipped the ball over the advancing goalkeeper with remarkable composure. At 17 years, 10 months, and 7 days old, he became the youngest goal scorer in Barcelona's history at that time.

7
THE FAMOUS NUMBER 10

In football, the number 10 jersey is traditionally reserved for the team's most creative and influential player, often the playmaker or star attacker. At FC Barcelona, this number was previously worn by legends such as Diego Maradona and Ronaldinho. In 2008, when Ronaldinho departed the club, Messi inherited the iconic number 10 shirt. This was more than a mere change in numbers; it was a symbolic passing of the torch.

8
WINNING THE BALLON D'OR

The Ballon d'Or is one of football's most prestigious individual awards, presented annually by France Football magazine to the best player in the world. Messi won his first Ballon d'Or in 2009 at the age of 22, following a sensational season where he helped Barcelona secure an unprecedented sextuple—winning six major trophies in one year. He received the award with a record-breaking margin, securing over 90% of the votes, highlighting his dominance in the sport. As of 2024, Messi has won the Ballon d'Or a record eight times, more than any other player in history.

9

A RECORD-BREAKING YEAR

In 2012, Messi achieved an extraordinary feat by scoring 91 goals in a single calendar year, surpassing the previous record of 85 goals set by German striker Gerd Müller in 1972. His goals came across various competitions, including La Liga, the UEFA Champions League, Copa del Rey, and international matches with Argentina. This remarkable achievement showcased his relentless scoring ability and consistency at the highest levels of competition.

10
THE TREBLE WITH BARCELONA

In the 2008-2009 season, Messi was instrumental in leading FC Barcelona to win the treble, a rare achievement where a club wins its domestic league, main national cup, and the primary continental competition in the same season. Under the guidance of manager Pep Guardiola, Barcelona won La Liga, the Copa del Rey, and the UEFA Champions League. Messi played a crucial role, finishing as the top scorer in the Champions League with nine goals, including a memorable header in the final against Manchester United.

11
CAPTAIN OF ARGENTINA

In 2011, Messi was appointed as the captain of the Argentine national team, a role that carries immense responsibility and honor. Taking over from Javier Mascherano, he became the leader both on and off the pitch. As captain, Messi's role extended beyond his exceptional playing abilities; he was tasked with uniting the team, motivating his teammates, and representing his country on the global stage.

12

OLYMPIC GOLD MEDALIST

In 2008, Messi achieved one of his early international successes by winning a gold medal with Argentina at the Beijing Olympics. Initially, there was uncertainty about his participation, as FC Barcelona was reluctant to release him for the tournament. However, after discussions and Messi's expressed desire to represent his country, the club allowed him to join the Olympic squad. In the final against Nigeria, Argentina secured a 1-0 victory, with Messi setting up the winning goal. Winning the Olympic gold marked his first major international honor.

13
CHARITY WORK

Off the pitch, Messi is known for his philanthropic efforts, particularly through the Leo Messi Foundation, which he established in 2007. The foundation focuses on providing access to education, health care, and sports opportunities for vulnerable children worldwide. Inspired by his own experiences and challenges during childhood, Messi is committed to helping those in need.

14
A FAMILY MAN

Messi is married to Antonela Roccuzzo, his childhood sweetheart whom he has known since he was five years old. Antonela is also from Rosario, and their families have been friends for many years. The couple began dating in 2008 and married in a lavish ceremony in Rosario in 2017, often referred to as the "wedding of the century" in Argentina. Together, they have three sons: Thiago (born in 2012), Mateo (born in 2015), and Ciro (born in 2018).

Messi is an avid animal lover and has a special affection for dogs. He owns a massive Dogue de Bordeaux named Hulk, who has become somewhat of a celebrity himself through appearances on Messi's social media. Hulk joined the Messi family in 2016 as a puppy and quickly grew into a gigantic companion. Messi often shares videos of himself playing football with Hulk in their backyard, demonstrating the dog's playful attempts to chase the ball.

16
THE LEFT-FOOTED WONDER

Messi is renowned for his incredible left foot, which is considered one of the most potent weapons in football history. His left-footed shots, passes, and dribbles are executed with remarkable precision and finesse. From bending free-kicks into the top corner to threading intricate passes through tight defenses, his left foot has delivered countless memorable moments. Despite being naturally left-footed, Messi has worked diligently to improve his right foot over the years, making him a more versatile and unpredictable player.

17
RECORD HOLDER FOR GOALS IN LA LIGA

Messi holds the record for the most goals scored in La Liga, the top professional football division of the Spanish football league system. He surpassed the previous record held by Telmo Zarra, who scored 251 goals in the 1940s and 1950s. As of his last season with Barcelona, Messi had scored over 450 La Liga goals, a testament to his longevity and consistency. His scoring record includes multiple seasons where he was the league's top scorer, earning him several Pichichi Trophies.

18
THE FIVE-GOAL MATCH

On March 7, 2012, Messi made history by scoring five goals in a single UEFA Champions League match against Bayer Leverkusen. The game ended in a 7-1 victory for Barcelona, with Messi's performance drawing widespread acclaim. He became the first player ever to score five goals in a Champions League knockout stage match, showcasing his ability to dominate even at the highest levels of competition.

19
A COLLECTOR OF HAT-TRICKS

A hat-trick occurs when a player scores three goals in a single game, a significant achievement in football. Messi has scored over 50 hat-tricks in his professional career, including in La Liga, the Champions League, and international matches with Argentina. His ability to consistently deliver such performances sets him apart from his peers. Each hat-trick showcases his versatility and skill, with goals coming from open play, set-pieces, and penalties.

20
THE MESSI AND RONALDO RIVALRY

For over a decade, Messi and Portuguese forward Cristiano Ronaldo have been considered the two best footballers in the world, sparking a rivalry that has captivated fans globally. Their competition has been characterized by mutual respect and has pushed both players to reach unprecedented heights. Between them, they have won numerous individual awards, including multiple Ballon d'Or titles, and have broken countless records. Their contrasting styles—Messi's creative playmaking and dribbling versus Ronaldo's physicality and aerial prowess—have fueled many debates among supporters and analysts.

21
FIRST RED CARD

In a surprising and unfortunate start to his senior international career, Messi received a red card just 43 seconds into his debut for Argentina's national team on August 17, 2005. Coming on as a substitute in a friendly match against Hungary, he was sent off for allegedly elbowing an opponent who was tugging on his shirt. The decision was controversial and left Messi in tears as he left the field. Despite this rocky beginning, he didn't let it discourage him. Instead, he used it as motivation to work harder and prove himself on the international stage.

22
ELUSIVE WORLD CUP DREAMS

Messi played in his first FIFA World Cup in 2006 and has participated in several since then. His lifelong dream has been to win the World Cup with Argentina, the most prestigious tournament in international soccer. In 2014, he led Argentina to the World Cup final, but they narrowly lost to Germany. Despite the disappointment, Messi was awarded the Golden Ball as the tournament's best player. In his first 4 World Cups the trophy eluded him.

23
COPA AMÉRICA VICTORY

In 2021, Messi achieved a significant milestone by leading Argentina to win the Copa América, South America's premier international soccer tournament. This victory ended Argentina's 28-year wait for a major international trophy and was Messi's first major title with the senior national team. Throughout the tournament, he was in outstanding form, contributing four goals and five assists, and was named the Best Player of the tournament.

24
THE PSG CHAPTER

In August 2021, after spending 21 years with Barcelona, Messi moved to Paris Saint-Germain (PSG) in France. The transfer was a significant change in his career, marking the end of an era at Barcelona where he had become a club legend. At PSG, he joined former teammate Neymar Jr. and young star Kylian Mbappé, forming a formidable attacking trio. The move was prompted by financial constraints at Barcelona, making it impossible for the club to renew his contract.

25
THE NUMBER 30 JERSEY

At PSG, Messi chose to wear the number 30 jersey, returning to the number he wore when he first started his professional career at Barcelona. The number 10 jersey, which he famously wore at Barcelona, was already taken by Neymar Jr. Messi opted for number 30 as a nod to his early days and as a symbol of a new beginning. Fans embraced the change, and the number 30 PSG jerseys quickly became popular worldwide.

26
AMBASSADOR FOR UNICEF

Messi has been a Goodwill Ambassador for UNICEF, the United Nations Children's Fund, since 2010. In this role, he helps raise awareness and support for children's rights and welfare around the world. He has participated in campaigns promoting education, health care, and protection for vulnerable children. Messi has visited countries affected by natural disasters and conflicts, bringing attention to the needs of children in those regions.

27
THE MESSI STORE

In 2019, Messi launched his own clothing line called "The Messi Store." The brand offers sportswear and casual clothes that reflect his personal style and values. The collection includes high-quality apparel designed for comfort and performance, appealing to both athletes and fans. The venture is managed by his sister, María Sol Messi, highlighting the family's involvement in his business endeavors.

28
VIDEO GAME STAR

Messi has been featured on the cover of popular soccer video games like EA Sports' FIFA series and Konami's Pro Evolution Soccer (PES). Gamers love playing as Messi because of his amazing in-game skills, which mirror his real-life abilities. His character is often rated among the highest in the games, reflecting his status as one of the best players in the world. His presence in video games has helped him reach a younger audience and solidify his status as a global icon.

29
A RECORD SIX GOLDEN BOOTS

Messi has won the European Golden Boot award six times, more than any other player in history. This award is given annually to the top scorer in European leagues. His victories came in the 2009–10, 2011–12, 2012–13, 2016–17, 2017–18, and 2018–19 seasons. This achievement highlights his goal-scoring prowess and consistency over many seasons. Winning the Golden Boot multiple times showcases his ability to outperform other top scorers across Europe.

30
FRIENDSHIP WITH NEYMAR AND SUÁREZ

At Barcelona, Messi formed a famous attacking trio with teammates Neymar Jr. and Luis Suárez, known as "MSN." They were celebrated for their incredible teamwork, understanding, and friendship both on and off the field. Together, they led Barcelona to numerous victories, including a treble in the 2014–15 season, winning La Liga, Copa del Rey, and the UEFA Champions League. Their chemistry resulted in countless goals and assists, making them one of the most feared attacking units in soccer history. Off the field, they shared a close bond, often spending time together and supporting each other.

31
FIRST CONTRACT ON A NAPKIN

Believe it or not, Messi's first contract with Barcelona was written on a napkin! In December 2000, Carles Rexach, Barcelona's technical secretary, was so impressed with 13-year-old Messi's talent during a trial that he wanted to secure his signing immediately. Without official paper on hand, he grabbed a napkin and wrote down the terms of the agreement. This unusual contract marked the beginning of Messi's long and successful journey with the club. The napkin has since become a legendary piece of memorabilia.

32
THE YOUNGEST TO SCORE IN EL CLÁSICO

El Clásico is the legendary match between Spanish giants Barcelona and Real Madrid, one of the most anticipated fixtures in world football. On March 10, 2007, at just 19 years old, Messi became the youngest player to ever score in this historic rivalry. Not only did he score once, but he netted a hat-trick, with each goal equalizing the score in a thrilling 3-3 draw. His performance was sensational and announced his arrival on the biggest stage.

33
HIS FAVORITE MEAL

Messi's favorite food is Milanesa Napolitana, an Argentine dish made of breaded fried beef topped with tomato sauce, ham, and melted cheese. It's similar to a South American version of a schnitzel or chicken parmesan. Enjoying traditional foods helps him stay connected to his roots, no matter where he is in the world. His mother often prepared this dish for him during his childhood, and it's remained a comfort food throughout his life.

34
FEATURED IN CIRQUE DU SOLEIL

Cirque du Soleil, the famous Canadian entertainment company known for its spectacular acrobatic performances, created a show called "Messi10" inspired by his life and career. Premiering in 2019, the performance combines soccer and acrobatics to tell his story in a unique and entertaining way. The show features 10 sequences, each representing different aspects of Messi's journey, from his early days in Rosario to his record-breaking achievements.

35
A FAN OF PLAYSTATION

In his free time, Messi enjoys playing video games, especially on his PlayStation console. It's a fun way for him to relax and unwind after intense matches and training sessions. He often plays sports games and has mentioned enjoying the FIFA series, where he can play as himself or compete with friends online. Just like many kids around the world, he loves immersing himself in virtual adventures. His interest in gaming makes him relatable to fans and shows that despite his superstar status, he enjoys the same hobbies as many others.

TATTOOS WITH MEANING

Messi has several tattoos, each with special significance and personal meaning. He has a portrait of his mother, Celia, on his back, showing his gratitude and love for her support throughout his life. On his calf, he has the names and handprints of his sons, Thiago, Mateo, and Ciro, symbolizing his devotion to his family. He also has tattoos of important symbols like a rosary in the shape of his hometown, Rosario, and a lotus flower representing new beginnings. He also has a 'Five of Cups' card from the Spanish deck of cards to symbolize the main trophies he's won.

37
THE GOAL CELEBRATION

After scoring a goal, Messi often points both index fingers to the sky. This gesture is a tribute to his late grandmother, Celia, who was a big supporter of his soccer dreams and played a crucial role in his early development. She would accompany him to training and matches, encouraging him every step of the way. By dedicating his goals to her, Messi honors her memory and keeps her influence close to his heart.

38
STANDING TALL

Despite being only 5 feet 7 inches tall, Messi has scored important goals with his head, surprising opponents and fans alike. In the 2009 UEFA Champions League final against Manchester United, he scored a remarkable header over taller defenders, helping Barcelona secure a 2-0 victory. This goal was particularly memorable because heading is not typically his main strength, and it came at a crucial moment in a major match.

39
A RECORD
FOR ASSISTS

Messi doesn't just score goals; he's also renowned for his playmaking abilities and has provided countless assists to his teammates. He holds records for the most assists in La Liga and other competitions. His vision, creativity, and precise passing make him a constant threat, allowing him to set up scoring opportunities from almost anywhere on the pitch. His unselfish play and ability to read the game contribute significantly to his team's success.

40
LEARNING CATALAN

While living in Barcelona, Messi learned to speak Catalan, the local language of the region. This helped him connect with fans and teammates on a deeper level and shows his respect for the culture of his adopted home. Being multilingual also aids in communication on the field, allowing for better coordination with teammates.

Before joining Barcelona, Messi played for Newell's Old Boys, a club in his hometown of Rosario. He has expressed a desire to play for them again before he retires, honoring the club where his journey began. His loyalty to his roots is admired by fans worldwide. Newell's Old Boys hold a special place in his heart, and he has maintained connections with the club over the years. Returning to play for them would be a full-circle moment, bringing his career back to where it all started.

42

YOUNGEST ARGENTINE IN A WORLD CUP

At 18 years old, Messi became the youngest player to represent Argentina in a FIFA World Cup match during the 2006 tournament in Germany. He made his debut in a group stage match against Serbia and Montenegro, coming on as a substitute and quickly making an impact by providing an assist and scoring a goal in a 6-0 victory.

43
CROWNING OF THE G.O.A.T.

On December 18, 2022, Messi achieved his ultimate career goal by leading Argentina to victory in the FIFA World Cup held in Qatar. In a thrilling final against France that ended 3-3 after extra time, Messi scored twice and successfully converted his penalty in the shootout, helping Argentina win 4-2 on penalties. This monumental triumph fulfilled his lifelong dream and silenced any remaining doubts about his legacy. Lifting the World Cup trophy cemented his status as the "Greatest of All Time" (G.O.A.T.), completing his collection of major football honors and bringing immense joy to his nation.

44
THE "MESSI ZONE"

Opponents often talk about the "Messi Zone," referring to areas on the field where he is most dangerous and likely to create scoring opportunities. Coaches devise special strategies and tactics to try to stop him, but his ability to find space and exploit defenses makes him incredibly difficult to contain. His intelligence, agility, and technical skills allow him to navigate tight spaces and unlock even the most organized defenses. The concept of the "Messi Zone" highlights the respect and concern he commands from opposing teams, as they recognize the unique challenge he presents.

45
HONORED WITH A STATUE

A statue of Messi stands in Buenos Aires, Argentina, as part of the "Paseo de la Gloria" (Walk of Glory), honoring his contributions to soccer and his country. The monument captures him in action, symbolizing his dynamic presence on the field. This honor places him alongside other great Argentine athletes and serves as an inspiration to young players. The statue not only celebrates his achievements but also acknowledges the pride he brings to his nation. It stands as a testament to his impact on Argentine sports and culture.

46
NO 1 IN SIX DIFFERENT COMPETITIONS

In the 2011–12 season, Messi became the first Barcelona player to score in six different club competitions in a single season. This includes goals in La Liga, Copa del Rey, UEFA Champions League, Spanish Super Cup, UEFA Super Cup, and FIFA Club World Cup. His versatility and consistency across multiple tournaments highlight his exceptional talent. Achieving this feat showcases his ability to adapt to different competitions and opponents, contributing to his team's success on all fronts. It's another record that emphasizes his place among soccer's all-time greats.

47
HIS OWN THEME PARK

Plans were announced for a Messi-themed amusement park called "The Messi Experience Park" in China. The park aims to combine soccer and entertainment, allowing fans to immerse themselves in interactive experiences inspired by his life and career. Attractions would include virtual and augmented reality exhibits, skill challenges, and educational elements about health and sportsmanship. As of 2024, the park is yet to open.

48
A PASSION FOR MUSIC

Messi enjoys listening to music, especially songs from his home country of Argentina. Music helps him relax and stay connected to his roots, providing comfort during his travels and busy schedule. He has mentioned enjoying genres like cumbia and reggaeton, and certain songs remind him of his childhood and family. Music plays a role in his pre-game routine, helping him focus and prepare mentally for matches. His passion for music adds another dimension to his personality and shows how he balances his professional life with personal interests.

49
THE MESSI BRAND OF WINE

A winery in Argentina produces a line of wines called "Leo," with proceeds supporting his foundation. The wines are made in collaboration with Bodega Valentin Bianchi, a well-respected Argentine winery. This venture combines his interest in business with his commitment to charity, contributing to causes he cares about. The "Leo" wines offer fans a way to support his philanthropic efforts while enjoying a product that represents his heritage. This initiative reflects his desire to give back and leverage his fame for positive impact.

50 MEETING THE POPE

Messi, a fellow Argentine, had the opportunity to meet Pope Francis at the Vatican. The meeting was a special moment connecting two influential figures from Argentina who share a passion for promoting peace and helping others. They discussed topics like sportsmanship, social responsibility, and the role of soccer in uniting people. The encounter was celebrated by fans around the world and highlighted the mutual respect between them. Meeting the Pope was a significant personal experience for Messi, reflecting his values and the respect he holds for spiritual and community leaders.

51
PABLO AIMAR
SPORTING HERO

Growing up, Messi idolized fellow Argentine footballer Pablo Aimar. He admired Aimar's creativity and skill on the pitch, often trying to imitate his playing style during his own games. Meeting his childhood hero later in life was a dream come true for Messi, and they even played against each other professionally. This admiration inspired him during his formative years and contributed to the development of his own unique style.

52
"GOAL OF THE CENTURY" REPLICA

In 2007, Messi scored an incredible goal against Getafe that mirrored Diego Maradona's famous "Goal of the Century" from the 1986 World Cup. He dribbled past multiple defenders, covering over half the length of the pitch before slotting the ball into the net. This goal drew worldwide attention and comparisons to Maradona, highlighting Messi's extraordinary talent and cementing his place among the greats.

53
MOST CONSECUTIVE MATCHES SCORED IN

During the 2012-2013 season, Messi set a record by scoring in 21 consecutive La Liga matches. This remarkable streak showcased his consistency and ability to perform at a high level week after week. Scoring 33 goals during this run, he demonstrated an unparalleled level of excellence that contributed significantly to Barcelona's success that season.

54
YOUNGEST TO WIN THREE BALLON D'ORS

By the age of 24, Messi had already won three Ballon d'Or awards, making him the youngest player ever to achieve this feat. His early and rapid accumulation of accolades set him apart from his peers. This accomplishment highlighted his dominance in the sport and predicted the continued success he would enjoy in his career.

55
COVID-19 CHARITY

In response to the COVID-19 pandemic, Messi made significant donations to hospitals in Argentina and Spain. He provided funds for medical equipment, research, and support for healthcare workers on the front lines. His generosity during this critical time demonstrated his compassion and commitment to helping those in need beyond the realm of sports.

56
THE MESSI EMOJI

In 2016, to celebrate the Copa América Centenario, Twitter created a special emoji of Messi. Whenever users tweeted #Messi, a custom emoji of his face would appear next to the hashtag. This unique honor showcased his immense popularity on social media and engaged fans during the tournament in a fun and interactive way.

Messi holds the record for the most official appearances in matches for FC Barcelona. Surpassing previous legends like Xavi Hernández, he demonstrated his long-term commitment and loyalty to the club. Each appearance added to his legacy, making him an integral part of Barcelona's history. His record number of games played is a testament to his durability and dedication over many seasons.

58
SPORTS-MAD

While football is his primary passion, Messi has shown interest in other sports, such as basketball and tennis. He's been spotted attending NBA games and has expressed admiration for basketball stars like Kobe Bryant and LeBron James. His appreciation for various sports reflects his love for athleticism and competition. Engaging with different sports also helps him relax and draw inspiration from athletes in other disciplines.

59
THE MESSI-INSPIRED ADIDAS BOOTS

Adidas, his long-time sponsor, has released special edition football boots inspired by Messi. These boots often feature unique designs that commemorate significant milestones in his career. Fans and players alike enjoy wearing them, celebrating his influence on football fashion and gear. The limited-edition boots often sell out quickly, showing the high demand for products associated with him.

60
MESSI STAMPS AND CURRENCY

Messi's image has appeared on postage stamps and commemorative coins in different countries, including Argentina and Spain. These collectibles honor his achievements and allow fans to celebrate his legacy. Being featured on stamps and currency is a rare tribute that signifies his impact on a national and global scale. Collectors value these items as symbols of his storied career and contributions to the sport.

61
400 GOAL KING

Messi became the fastest player to score 400 goals in Europe's top five leagues. Achieving this milestone highlighted his prolific scoring ability and consistency at the highest levels of competition. His goal-scoring rate continues to set new benchmarks in football history. Reaching this number in fewer matches than any other player emphasizes his exceptional efficiency.

62
LAUREUS SPORTSMAN OF THE YEAR AWARD

In 2020, Messi won the prestigious Laureus World Sportsman of the Year award, sharing the honor with Formula 1 driver Lewis Hamilton. He became the first footballer to receive this award, recognizing his excellence and significant impact on sports globally. The award celebrated not just his athletic achievements but also his sportsmanship and influence off the field.

63
THE MESSI BURGER

A famous restaurant chain collaborated with Messi to create the "Messi Burger," featuring his favorite ingredients. Fans can enjoy this special meal, connecting with their idol through a shared love of food. It's a fun and tasty way to celebrate his influence beyond the football field. The burger's popularity reflects his widespread appeal and the joy he brings to fans in various ways.

64
HIS OWN SIGNATURE TYPEFACE

Adidas developed a custom font called "Messi," used in marketing materials and his official merchandise. The typeface reflects his personal brand and style, adding a unique touch to his endorsements. This innovation showcases his influence in design and branding within sports. The font has become recognizable among fans, further solidifying his personal brand identity.

65
HONORARY CITIZEN
OF BANGLADESH

Due to his immense popularity and the passionate fan base in Bangladesh, Messi was named an honorary citizen of the country. His ability to unite fans across different cultures and nations demonstrates the universal appeal of his talent and sportsmanship. This honor reflects the deep admiration people around the world have for him, transcending borders.

66
FAN OF THE HARRY POTTER SERIES

Messi enjoys reading and has expressed a fondness for the "Harry Potter" books. He appreciates the themes of friendship, bravery, and perseverance found in the stories. This interest connects him with young fans who also love the magical world created by J.K. Rowling. Reading these books allows him to relax and escape into imaginative adventures off the pitch.

67
THE MESSI-THEMED PRIVATE JET

In 2018, Messi acquired a private jet customized with personal touches, including his iconic number 10 and the names of his family members on the steps. The jet serves as a comfortable means for him to travel for matches and personal commitments, reflecting his success and focus on family. The personalized aircraft also symbolizes his journey and the importance he places on staying connected with loved ones.

68
MOST GOALS
WITH ONE CLUB

Messi holds the Guinness World Record for the most goals scored for a single club, surpassing the legendary Pelé's long-standing record. This achievement underscores his loyalty and incredible contribution to FC Barcelona over his illustrious career. Breaking Pelé's record solidified his place among the greatest footballers of all time.

69
HIS SON PLAYS FOOTBALL TOO

Messi's eldest son, Thiago, has started following in his father's footsteps by playing football. Enrolled in Inter Miami's youth academy, Thiago shows enthusiasm for the sport. Messi supports his son's interest, often attending his matches and sharing tips, passing the love of the game to the next generation. It's heartwarming to see the football legacy continue within his family.

Outside of football, Messi has an interest in automobiles and owns a collection of luxury cars, including Ferraris, Maseratis, and Audis. His appreciation for design and engineering is reflected in his selection of vehicles. This hobby provides him with enjoyment off the pitch. His car collection also showcases his success and personal tastes.

71
FROM RIVALS TO TEAMMATES

For many years, Messi and Spanish defender Sergio Ramos were fierce rivals in the legendary El Clásico matches between FC Barcelona and Real Madrid. In a surprising turn of events, both players joined Paris Saint-Germain (PSG) in 2021, becoming teammates for the first time. Their collaboration at PSG showcased their professionalism and ability to set aside past rivalries for the good of the team. Fans were excited to see these two football legends play together, adding a new and unexpected chapter to their storied careers.

72

NAMED THE BEST PLAYMAKER BY IFFHS

The International Federation of Football History & Statistics (IFFHS) has named Messi the World's Best Playmaker multiple times. This award recognizes his exceptional ability to create scoring opportunities, not just for himself but also for his teammates, highlighting his all-around brilliance on the field. His vision and creativity set him apart as a true maestro of the game.

73
RECORD DRIBBLER IN A WORLD CUP

In the 2014 FIFA World Cup, Messi set a record for the most successful dribbles in a single tournament. His ability to weave through defenders dazzled audiences worldwide and was a key factor in Argentina reaching the final. His dribbling skills are a defining aspect of his playing style. This performance further enhanced his reputation as one of the most skilled dribblers ever.

74
RECIPIENT OF THE GOLDEN FOOT AWARD

In 2019, Messi received the Golden Foot Award, which honors players over the age of 28 for their athletic achievements and personality. Unlike other awards, the Golden Foot can only be won once, making it a unique accolade in his collection. His footprints were immortalized on "The Champions Promenade" in Monaco. This honor recognizes both his football excellence and his character off the field.

75
A FAN OF "GAME OF THRONES"

Messi has expressed his enjoyment of the popular television series "Game of Thrones." He followed the show's complex storylines and characters, discussing episodes with friends and teammates. This interest shows that he, like many others, enjoys immersing himself in epic tales during his downtime. It also provides common ground for conversations outside of football.

76
HIS CHARITY BUILT A CANCER CENTER

Messi's foundation contributed significant funds to help build the SJD Pediatric Cancer Center in Barcelona. This state-of-the-art facility focuses on treating and researching childhood cancer. His support provides hope and resources to countless children and their families facing serious health challenges. The center stands as a testament to his commitment to making a lasting, positive impact.

77
MOST GOALS IN A LEAGUE SEASON

During the 2011–2012 La Liga season, Messi scored an astonishing 50 goals, setting a record for the most goals in a single season in any of Europe's top leagues. This remarkable achievement highlighted his exceptional talent and goal-scoring prowess, contributing greatly to Barcelona's success. His record-breaking season remains one of the most prolific in football history.

78
ENVIRONMENTAL CAUSES

Messi supports environmental initiatives and has participated in campaigns promoting sustainability and conservation. As a UNICEF Goodwill Ambassador, he has been involved in efforts to raise awareness about the impact of climate change on vulnerable children worldwide. He has supported UNICEF's "Raise Your Voice Against Climate Change" campaign, encouraging global action to protect the environment for future generations. He understands the importance of protecting the planet and uses his platform to advocate for environmental responsibility.

79
THE MESSI SPORTS CENTER IN ROSARIO

In his hometown of Rosario, Messi funded the construction of a sports complex called "Complejo Deportivo." The facility provides opportunities for local youth to engage in sports and develop their talents. This project allows him to give back to the community that nurtured his early passion for football. The center serves as an inspiration for young athletes pursuing their dreams.

80
ICONIC MADRID GOAL CELEBRATION

In April 2017, after scoring a last-minute winning goal against Real Madrid, Messi celebrated by holding up his Barcelona jersey to the crowd at the Santiago Bernabéu Stadium. This iconic moment became one of the most memorable celebrations in football history, symbolizing his impact on the fierce rivalry. The image of him displaying his jersey is etched in the memories of football fans worldwide.

81
TWO TIME WINNER
OF GOLDEN BALL

Messi made history by becoming the first player ever to win the Golden Ball award twice at the FIFA World Cup. He first received this prestigious honor in 2014, recognizing him as the best player of the tournament when Argentina reached the final. He won it again in 2022 after leading Argentina to victory and lifting the World Cup trophy. This remarkable achievement highlights his consistent excellence on football's biggest stage and cements his legacy as one of the greatest players in World Cup history. Winning the Golden Ball twice showcases his ability to perform at the highest level over many years.

82
MESSI-INSPIRED DANCE MOVES

Fans around the world have created dance moves and routines inspired by Messi's agility and footwork on the pitch. These dances often go viral on social media platforms, showcasing the joy and creativity he inspires beyond football. They celebrate his influence in a fun and engaging way that transcends language and culture.

83
SPECIAL OLYMPICS AMBASSADOR

Messi has served as a global ambassador for the Special Olympics, promoting inclusion and support for athletes with intellectual disabilities. He advocates for the transformative power of sports to empower individuals and break down barriers. His involvement brings attention to the importance of acceptance and equal opportunities in athletics.

84
THE MESSI HEADBAND

Early in his career, Messi often wore a headband during matches to keep his longer hair in place. This distinctive look became popular among young fans who wanted to emulate his style on the field. The headband became a part of his early image as he rose to fame. It also highlighted his youthful exuberance during his breakout years.

85
FEATURED IN A COMIC BOOK

Messi's life story has been adapted into comic books and graphic novels aimed at younger audiences. These publications illustrate his journey from a small boy in Rosario to an international football superstar, inspiring kids with themes of perseverance and dedication. The comics make his story accessible and engaging for children who look up to him.

86
22 minute
HAT-TRICK

In 2016, Messi scored a hat-trick in just 22 minutes during a Champions League match against Celtic. This rapid trio of goals showcased his ability to take control of a game swiftly, leaving opponents little time to react and thrilling fans with his brilliance. His performance set a new standard for efficiency in goal scoring at the highest level.

BONUS!
Watch **all** of Messi's Champions League goals by scanning the QR code above

87
MULTIPLE UEFA GOALS OF THE SEASON

Messi has won the UEFA Goal of the Season award multiple times for his spectacular strikes in European competitions. Fans vote for their favorite goals, and his consistently make the list due to their skillful execution and importance in big matches. These awards highlight his knack for delivering when it matters most.

88
THE MESSI TRAINING APP

A mobile application was developed featuring Messi's training routines and skill challenges. Fans and aspiring players can use the app to practice drills, improve their techniques, and learn from one of the best. It's an interactive way for him to connect with supporters and promote the sport. The app encourages healthy activity and skill development among users.

89
HIS OWN THEME SONG

"La Pulga" is admired by his fans in his native country who have come up with a special chant for the Inter Miami forward. The Lionel Messi chant is popularly known as 'De la mano de Leo Messi', referring to a phrase in the chant which means 'hand in hand with Leo Messi'. It means, "Come, come, sing with me, you're gonna find a friend, and by the hand of Leo Messi. We are going to run all over the field."

BONUS!
Watch Messi's Argentinian teammates sing him the song after winning the Finalissima in 2022!

90
THE MESSI-INSPIRED ARTWORK

Artists worldwide have created murals, paintings, and sculptures of Messi, often displayed in public spaces. These works of art honor his contributions to football and culture, serving as inspiration and beautifying communities with his image. The artwork reflects the global admiration for his skills and character. The most famous ones are in his hometown of Rosario.

91
16 SEASON UCL SCORING STREAK

Messi made history by becoming the first player to score in 16 consecutive UEFA Champions League seasons. Starting from the 2005–06 season and continuing through to the 2020–21 season, he consistently found the back of the net against Europe's elite clubs. This remarkable achievement highlights his longevity and sustained excellence at the highest level of club football. His ability to perform consistently in such a demanding competition underscores his status as The G.O.A.T.

92
ACCESSIBILITY PARTNERSHIP

Messi partnered with OrCam Technologies, a company that develops devices to assist visually impaired individuals. As a global ambassador, he promotes their innovative technology, helping to raise awareness and improve the lives of people with vision challenges. His support brings attention to the importance of accessibility and inclusion.

Messi expanded his business ventures into the hospitality industry by investing in a chain of hotels known as MiM Hotels. Located in popular Spanish destinations like Sitges, Ibiza, Mallorca, and the ski resort of Baqueira, these luxury hotels offer premium accommodations and services. Operated by Majestic Hotel Group, the properties reflect Messi's interest in tourism and business beyond football. His investment in the hotel industry showcases his entrepreneurial spirit and planning for life after his playing career, diversifying his portfolio and contributing to the hospitality sector.

94
A FAN OF
BOARD GAMES

Messi enjoys playing board games like Monopoly and Parcheesi with his family. These games offer him a way to relax and spend quality time with loved ones away from the spotlight. His fondness for simple pleasures reflects his down-to-earth personality. Family game nights help him maintain a strong bond with his children, showing that even the greatest football stars cherish ordinary moments with their families.

95
A RECORD-BREAKING SOCIAL MEDIA POST

After winning the FIFA World Cup in 2022, Messi shared a celebratory photo on Instagram that became the most-liked post by an athlete on the platform. The image showed him lifting the World Cup trophy, and it quickly amassed over 70 million likes, surpassing previous records. This achievement highlights not only his immense popularity but also the global impact of his World Cup victory. The overwhelming response demonstrates how Messi's accomplishments resonate with millions of people around the world, transcending sports to become a significant cultural moment.

96
RECORD FOR MOST WINS WITH BARÇA

During his time at Barcelona, Messi amassed more victories than any other player in the club's history. His contributions led to numerous trophies and championships, including multiple La Liga titles and UEFA Champions League victories. His winning mentality and leadership were instrumental in Barcelona's golden era, where the team was known for its beautiful style of play and dominance. Messi's dedication to his club over more than two decades showcased his loyalty and passion for the game. His record number of wins highlights not just his individual talent but also his ability to elevate his team to success, making him a true legend at the club.

97
GLOBAL ADVERTISING CAMPAIGNS

Messi has appeared in advertisements for major global brands like Pepsi, Gatorade, Adidas, and Turkish Airlines. His endorsements extend his influence into marketing and popular culture, making him a familiar face even to those who may not follow football closely. His global appeal makes him a sought-after figure in the advertising world, often starring in creative and memorable commercials. These campaigns have taken him around the world, connecting with fans from different cultures and backgrounds.

Known for his humility, Messi often mentors younger teammates, offering advice and encouragement both on and off the field. His leadership helps develop their skills and confidence, and he is respected not only for his talent but also for his willingness to support others. His guidance fosters a positive team environment and nurtures future stars. Players like Ansu Fati and Pedri have benefited from his mentorship during their early careers at Barcelona. By sharing his experience and wisdom, Messi helps ensure that the next generation of footballers continues to grow and succeed, carrying forward the spirit of the game.

99
MOST APPEARANCES IN COPA AMÉRICA

Messi holds the record for the most appearances in the Copa América tournament for Argentina (36 as of 2024). His dedication to representing his country is evident in his long-standing participation and consistent performances in South America's premier competition. His commitment has earned him admiration from fans and peers alike. Throughout his Copa América career, he has provided crucial goals and assists, leading Argentina to victory in the 2021 and 2024 editions of the tournament.

100
LIMITED EDITION
MESSI WATCH

Jacob & Co. released a limited-edition timepiece inspired by Messi, featuring his signature and design elements related to his career. This collector's item is sought after by fans and watch enthusiasts, symbolizing his partnership with high-end brands. The watch represents the fusion of sport and luxury in his personal brand, combining elegance with athletic inspiration. Some editions incorporate his jersey number, favorite colors, or even materials related to football.

101
THE MESSI
ALGORITHM

Scientists and researchers have studied Messi's playing style to develop computer algorithms that analyze football tactics and player movements. His unique approach to dribbling and decision-making on the pitch has contributed to advancements in sports science and technology, showcasing the blend of art and data in modern football. These studies highlight how his natural talent can inform training methods and tactical analysis. By examining his movements and patterns, coaches and analysts aim to understand what makes him so effective, potentially improving training programs for aspiring players.

LEO TRIVIA

1. Where was Lionel Messi born?
A. Buenos Aires, Argentina
B. Rosario, Argentina
C. Madrid, Spain
D. Barcelona, Spain

2. What is Lionel Messi's famous nickname?
A. El Toro (The Bull)
B. El Maestro (The Master)
C. La Pulga (The Flea)
D. El Mago (The Magician)

3. At what age did Messi move to Barcelona to join their youth academy?
A. 10
B. 13
C. 15
D. 17

4. What medical condition was Messi diagnosed with as a child?
A. Asthma
B. Diabetes
C. Growth hormone deficiency
D. Heart murmur

5. On which item was Messi's first contract with Barcelona famously written?
A. A napkin
B. A match ticket
C. A piece of cardboard
D. A restaurant menu

6. At what age did Messi make his official debut for Barcelona's first team?
A. 16
B. 17
C. 18
D. 19

7. Who assisted Messi's first official goal for Barcelona?
A. Xavi Hernández
B. Andrés Iniesta
C. Ronaldinho
D. Samuel Eto'o

8. Which jersey number did Messi inherit from Ronaldinho at Barcelona?
A. 7
B. 9
C. 10
D. 11

9. How many Ballon d'Or awards has Messi won?
A. 5
B. 6
C. 7
D. 8

10. In what year did Messi score 91 goals in a single calendar year?
A. 2010
B. 2011
C. 2012
D. 2013

11. Which team did Messi help Argentina defeat to win the 2021 Copa América?
A. Brazil
B. Chile
C. Uruguay
D. Colombia

12. What is the name of Messi's wife?
A. Antonela Roccuzzo
B. Shakira
C. Georgina Rodríguez
D. Sofia Balbi

13. What is the name of Messi's giant dog?
A. Hulk
B. Thor
C. Zeus
D. Rocky

14. Which foot is Messi predominantly known for using?
A. Left foot
B. Right foot
C. Both equally
D. Neither; he's ambidextrous

15. Which club did Messi join in 2021 after leaving Barcelona?
A. Manchester City
B. Paris Saint-Germain (PSG)
C. Juventus
D. Inter Miami

16. What jersey number did Messi choose at PSG?
A. 10
B. 7
C. 19
D. 30

17. Which charitable organization is Messi a Goodwill Ambassador for?
A. UNICEF
B. UNESCO
C. World Health Organization
D. Amnesty International

18. What is the name of Messi's clothing line?
A. Messi Wear
B. The Messi Store
C. Leo Apparel
D. Messi Fashion

19. How many European Golden Boot awards has Messi won?
A. 4
B. 5
C. 6
D. 7

20. What was Lionel Messi's first major international trophy with Argentina?
A. FIFA World Cup
B. Copa América
C. Olympic Gold Medal
D. FIFA U-20 World Cup

21. Which dish is Messi's favorite food?
A. Paella
B. Milanesa Napolitana
C. Empanadas
D. Pizza Margherita

22. Which Cirque du Soleil show was inspired by Messi's life?
A. Messi10
B. Cirque Messi
C. The Magician
D. Goalkeeper

23. What is the name of Messi's foundation?
A. Leo Messi Foundation
B. Messi Kids Foundation
C. Lionel's Legacy
D. Football for Hope

24. Against which team did Messi score five goals in a single Champions League match?
A. Real Madrid
B. Arsenal
C. Bayer Leverkusen
D. Manchester City

25. Which language did Messi learn while living in Barcelona besides Spanish?
A. French
B. Italian
C. Catalan
D. Portuguese

26. Which Argentine club did Messi play for before joining Barcelona?
A. River Plate
B. Boca Juniors
C. Newell's Old Boys
D. Independiente

27. How does Messi often celebrate his goals?
A. Backflip
B. Pointing to the sky
C. Sliding on knees
D. Taking off his shirt

28. Which number did Messi wear when he first started his professional career at Barcelona?
A. 19
B. 10
C. 30
D. 7

29. What is the name of the theme park announced in China based on Messi?
A. Messi World
B. The Messi Experience Park
C. Lionel's Land
D. Goal Park

30. In what year did Messi win an Olympic gold medal with Argentina?
A. 2004
B. 2008
C. 2012
D. 2016

31. Who was Messi's football idol growing up?
A. Diego Maradona
B. Gabriel Batistuta
C. Pablo Aimar
D. Juan Román Riquelme

32. Which record did Messi break by scoring 50 goals in a La Liga season?
A. Most headed goals in a season
B. Most goals in a European league season
C. Most appearances in a season
D. Most hat-tricks in a season

33. In which year did Messi win his first Ballon d'Or?
A. 2008
B. 2009
C. 2010
D. 2011

34. In which year did Messi make his debut for Argentina's senior national team?
A. 2003
B. 2004
C. 2005
D. 2006

35. How many sons does Messi have?
A. One
B. Two
C. Three
D. Four

36. Which player is Messi often compared to for his dribble against Getafe in 2007?
A. Zinedine Zidane
B. Diego Maradona
C. Pelé
D. Cristiano Ronaldo

37. Which video game series has featured Messi on its cover?
A. FIFA
B. Pro Evolution Soccer (PES)
C. Both FIFA and PES
D. Neither FIFA nor PES

38. Which luxury watch brand released a limited-edition timepiece inspired by Messi?
A. Rolex
B. Omega
C. Jacob & Co.
D. Tag Heuer

39. What role does Messi's sister play in his clothing line?
A. She designs the clothes
B. She models the apparel
C. She manages the venture
D. She is the brand ambassador

40. Which award did Messi win for his sportsmanship and positive influence on the game?
A. FIFA Fair Play Award
B. Golden Foot Award
C. UEFA Best Player in Europe
D. Laureus Sportsman of the Year

41. What significant achievement did Messi accomplish by winning the FIFA World Cup in 2022?
A. First player to win five Ballon d'Or awards
B. Completed his collection of major football honors
C. Became the highest goal scorer in World Cup history
D. Retired from international football

42. Messi is the first player to win the Golden Ball award twice at the FIFA World Cup. In which years did he achieve this?
A. 2010 and 2014
B. 2014 and 2018
C. 2014 and 2022
D. 2018 and 2022

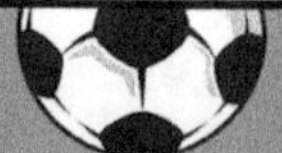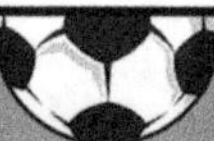

43. On what date did Messi lead Argentina to win the FIFA World Cup in Qatar?
A. July 15, 2018
B. December 18, 2022
C. June 12, 2014
D. November 21, 2022

44. What was unique about Messi's first appearance for Argentina's senior national team?
A. He scored a hat-trick
B. He was sent off after 43 seconds
C. He captained the team
D. He wore the number 10 jersey

45. Which wine brand is associated with Messi, with proceeds supporting his foundation?
A. Leo
B. Messi Vineyards
C. La Pulga Wines
D. Rosario Reserve

46. Which NBA players has Messi expressed admiration for?
A. Michael Jordan and Magic Johnson
B. Kobe Bryant and LeBron James
C. Stephen Curry and Kevin Durant
D. Shaquille O'Neal and Tim Duncan

47. Which team did Messi and his family support in his hometown?
A. River Plate
B. Boca Juniors
C. Newell's Old Boys
D. San Lorenzo

48. Which award did Messi receive at the 2014 FIFA World Cup?
A. Golden Boot
B. Golden Ball
C. Golden Glove
D. Best Young Player

49. What is the name of Messi's hotel chain?
A. MiM Hotels
B. Messi Inns
C. Leo Lodgings
D. Barcelona Suites

50. Which team did Messi help Argentina defeat in the 2022 FIFA World Cup final?
A. Germany
B. France
C. Brazil
D. Croatia

Answers

1. B. Rosario, Argentina
2. C. La Pulga (The Flea)
3. B. 13
4. C. Growth hormone deficiency
5. A. A napkin
6. B. 17
7. C. Ronaldinho
8. C. 10
9. D. 8
10. C. 2012
11. A. Brazil
12. A. Antonela Roccuzzo
13. A. Hulk
14. A. Left foot
15. B. Paris Saint-Germain (PSG)
16. D. 30
17. A. UNICEF
18. B. The Messi Store
19. C. 6
20. C. Olympic Gold Medal
21. B. Milanesa Napolitana
22. A. Messi10

23. A. Leo Messi Foundation
24. C. Bayer Leverkusen
25. C. Catalan
26. C. Newell's Old Boys
27. B. Pointing to the sky
28. C. 30
29. B. The Messi Experience Park
30. B. 2008
31. C. Pablo Aimar
32. B. Most goals in a European league season
33. B. 2009
34. C. 2005
35. C. Three
36. B. Diego Maradona
37. C. Both FIFA and PES
38. C. Jacob & Co.
39. C. She manages the venture
40. D. Laureus Sportsman of the Year
41. B. Completed his collection of major football honors
42. C. 2014 and 2022
43. B. December 18, 2022
44. B. He was sent off after 43 seconds
45. A. Leo
46. B. Kobe Bryant and LeBron James
47. C. Newell's Old Boys
48. B. Golden Ball
49. A. MiM Hotels
50. B. France

MESSI QUOTES

1. "You have to fight to reach your dream. You have to sacrifice and work hard for it."
Messi emphasizes the importance of perseverance and hard work in achieving one's goals.

2. "The best decisions aren't made with your mind, but with your instinct."
Highlighting the role of intuition and natural ability in making crucial choices on and off the field.

3. "There are more important things in life than winning or losing a game."
Messi underscores the value of humility and perspective beyond sports achievements.

4. "I start early, and I stay late, day after day, year after year. It took me 17 years and 114 days to become an overnight success."
A testament to his dedication and the long journey behind his success.

5. "You can overcome anything, if and only if you love something enough."
Messi speaks to the power of passion in overcoming challenges.

6. "The day you think there is no improvements to be made is a sad one for any player."
Emphasizing the importance of continuous growth and self-improvement.

7. "I don't need the best clothes or the most expensive cars. I'm happy with the simplest things."
Reflecting his humble nature and appreciation for simplicity despite his fame.

8. "I play for the pride of representing my country."
Expressing his deep sense of national pride and responsibility when playing for Argentina.

9. "You have to fight to reach your dream. You have to sacrifice and work hard for it."
A reminder of the relentless effort required to achieve one's aspirations.

10. "There is no better feeling than winning with the team when you've put your heart into it."
Highlighting the joy of collective success and teamwork.

11. "I have fun like a child in the street."
Describing his genuine enjoyment and love for the game of football.

12. "Sometimes you have to accept you can't win all the time."
Acknowledging the reality of setbacks and the importance of resilience.

13. "You have to take the chance when you have the chance."
Encouraging seizing opportunities when they arise, both in sports and life.

14. "I always think about winning, because that's what drives me."
Focusing on the motivation behind his relentless pursuit of victory.

15. "The truth is that I have more respect for the person who works hard to win than the one who is good but doesn't work hard."
Valuing dedication and effort over innate talent alone.

QUOTES ON MESSI

1. Cristiano Ronaldo on Messi:
"Messi is an incredible player and a true competitor. I admire his dedication and his ability to perform consistently at the highest level."

2. Diego Maradona on Messi:
"Messi is the greatest player the world has seen so far."

3. Pep Guardiola on Messi:
"Messi is the best player in the world. I have never seen someone play like him."

4. Johan Cruyff on Messi:
"Messi is the closest thing we have to a perfect footballer."

5. Andrés Iniesta on Messi:
"Messi is one of the greatest players ever to play the game."

6. Neymar Jr. on Messi:
"Messi is a true genius on the field. Playing alongside him has been a remarkable experience."

7. Xavi Hernández on Messi:
"Messi has everything to be considered the greatest of all time."

8. Zinedine Zidane on Messi:
"Messi is a phenomenal player and the best I have ever seen."

9. Samuel Eto'o on Messi:
"Messi is the greatest player to ever grace the game."

10. Frank Lampard on Messi:
"Messi is a phenomenal player who has changed football."

11. Marcelo Bielsa on Messi:
"Messi is the best player I've ever seen."

12. Zlatan Ibrahimović on Messi:
"Messi is a great player and one of the best ever."

13. Carles Puyol on Messi:
"Messi is the best player I've ever played with."

14. Manuel Pellegrini on Messi:
"Messi is a special player who has an incredible impact on the team."

15. Gary Lineker on Messi:
"Messi is an absolute magician on the field."

Wow, what an incredible journey we've had learning about Lionel Messi! From his amazing dribbling skills and record-breaking goals to his kind heart and dedication to helping others, we've uncovered so many fun and fascinating facts about his life. Messi's story shows us that with passion, hard work, and a big heart, we can achieve extraordinary things.

We've seen how Messi made history with his incredible performances on the field, led his team to countless victories, and even inspired young players around the world to chase their dreams. We've learned about his love for his family, his amazing collection of luxury cars, and how he supports important causes like education and health care. Every fact reveals a new side of Messi, making him even more inspiring.

As you close this book, remember that Messi's journey started with a dream and a lot of determination. We've left the next few pages blank so you can write down and journal what your biggest lessons from Lionel Messi are. Use this space to reflect on how Messi's journey inspires you and what dreams you want to achieve.

Thank you for joining us on this adventure through the life of Lionel Messi. We hope you've enjoyed discovering all these amazing facts. Now, go out there and make your own magic, just like Messi!

WHAT HAVE YOU LEARNED FROM MESSI?